Aisha Siddiqa عنها رضى الله

Sr. Nafees Khan
Toronto, Canada

Goodword

Aisha (ra), the wife of the Prophet Muhammad (pbuh), is an exemplary figure in the history of Islam. Historians see Aisha (ra) as a learned woman who tirelessly recorded the life of the Prophet Muhammad (pbuh) and explained Muslim history and traditions with intelligence and insight. She is considered to be one of the foremost scholars of the early Islamic age, with some historians giving her credit for one quarter of the Islamic sharia (Islamic religious laws) having been based on her hadith narrations. In various books of hadith, many of her judgments have been prescribed and are even now studied by Islamic scholars.

The life of Aisha (ra) is proof that a woman can be very learned and that she can be the teacher of scholars and experts. Her life is also a proof that a woman can influence men and women alike and provide them with inspiration and leadership.

Aisha (ra) was born at a time when a man would feel ashamed to become the father of a girl. That was a time when fathers would bury their daughters alive. Islam stopped this cruel practice and raised the position of women by giving them rights that they had never had before. Within a short period of time, Aisha (ra) received respect and great status due to her intelligence, knowledge, wisdom and other great admirable personal qualities, which shows the high regard there is for women in Islam.

Aisha (ra) was born in Makkah to Abu Bakr Siddiq (ra) and Umm Rumaan (ra), both of whom were amongst the first Makkans to accept Islam. Right from her birth she was raised in an Islamic environment.

She had one brother, Abdur Rahman, two step sisters and two step brothers. Their father was a successful businessman and belonged to the noble tribe of Quraish. Abu Bakr (ra) was known for his eloquence, intelligence and extensive knowledge. Of all his children, Aisha was the one who inherited her father's abilities to the greatest extent.

In the early part of her life, people noticed that she was not only pretty but was also a well-mannered and a talented little girl with an extraordinary memory. Aisha was very observant and always asked intelligent questions. If any ayaath (verses) of the Quran were recited in her presence, she would quickly memorize them. In other words, she was an extremely gifted child with a remarkable memory.

Abu Bakr's (ra) passion for Islam caused him to become the object of persecution. Nevertheless, he bravely persevered in maintaining his faith. His commitment to Islam had a great influence on Aisha (ra). From early childhood, she learned that one has to stand up for the truth and strive for a noble cause.

A decade after his mission started, the Prophet Muhammad (pbuh) was having a very difficult time. He was extremely sad after the deaths of his wife Khadijah (ra) and his uncle Abu Talib. Both were his strongest supporters and passed away within a short period of each other. The Prophet (pbuh) was also concerned, because the persecution of the Muslims by the Makkans had reached its peak.

Around this time, an angel appeared in a dream and presented him with a gift wrapped in silk. The Prophet (pbuh) asked the angel, "What is this?" The angel told him, "This is your wife!" When he unwrapped the silk, he saw an image of Aisha (ra). When he woke up the Prophet (pbuh) said to himself, "If this is from Allah, it will surely be!"

The Prophet (pbuh) discussed the matter with Khaulah (ra),the wife of a friend, and she approached Abu Bakr (ra) with the marriage proposal. Abu Bakr (ra) was thrilled.

A few days later, Aisha (ra) was married in a very simple ceremony conducted by Abu Bakr (ra) himself. She continued to live with her parents for the next three years; out of which the last nine months were spent in Madinah.

The Prophet Muhammad (pbuh) and Abu Bakr (ra) migrated to Madinah in 622 C.E., while their families stayed behind and waited until they were sent for. After some time the Prophet (pbuh) and Abu Bakr (ra) sent a few men to bring their families from Makkah. Abu Bakr's son, Abdullah, accompanied his mother and two sisters, Aisha and Asma (ra) on their journey to Madinah.

On the way to Madinah, the camel that was carrying Aisha (ra) started running out of control and created a dangerous situation. Umm Rumaan started crying, but Aisha (ra) kept her composure and held on tight. Everyone was relieved when the camel was brought under control after running for miles.

Due to the change in climate, many Muhajirs (immigrants), including Aisha (ra), fell ill in Madinah. Her illness was so severe that she lost her hair. When Aisha had recovered fully, her father suggested to the Prophet Muhammad (pbuh), that it was time for him to take her to his home. The Prophet (pbuh) told him that he had no money to give for her 'mahr' (dowry). Abu Bakr (ra) then offered to give him a loan of 500 dirhams, which he accepted and sent it to Aisha (ra). Her going away ceremony was simple. Thus she entered a holy environment where she received moral and spiritual training day and night directly from the Prophet (pbuh) himself.

Aisha's room was about 10 feet long with mud walls and floor. The roof was thatched with date leaves and was so low that one could easily touch it. The doorway opened into the Masjid un Nabi and a blanket was used as a curtain. The household items consisted of one bed, a mat, a pillow stuffed with date fibers, a water pitcher, a bowl and two earthen jars to store dates and flour.

This is the room where the Angel Jibreel (Gabriel) (pbuh) would descend with revelations from Allah (SWT) and once Aisha (ra) had the honour of seeing the Archangel in person.

While living with the Prophet Muhammad (pbuh) she underwent many hardships. Most of the times she could not get enough food to satisfy her hunger. For weeks at a time, the Prophet (pbuh) and his family did not have any cooked food. Yet, Aisha (ra) was content and did not complain.

Aisha (ra) narrated that the Prophet Muhammad's family did not have their fill of barley bread for three consecutive days till he died.

Aisha (ra) once told to Arwa bin Zubair, her nephew, 'Sometimes, for three long months, we never cooked anything in our house because we did not have anything during that period.' He then asked, 'how did you survive without it?' She replied, 'we used to eat dates and drink water or sometimes some of our neighbours used to send us some food and milk and the milk he used to give it to us.'

Abu Hurairah narrates, 'The family of the Prophet (pbuh) used to spend months without lighting a lamp and without cooking any meals as they would hardly ever had any olive oil.'

Aisha (ra) liked whatever her husband liked and disliked whatever he disliked. Once she hung a curtain on her doorway that had a picture of an animal on it. When the Prophet (pbuh) saw it, he got upset. Aisha (ra) was terrified and asked, "Please, Ya Rasool Allah, (Oh Messenger of God) what have I done to offend you?" Pointing to the curtain he said, "Angels do not enter a house that has pictures of men and animals!" She immediately took down the curtain.

She was very devoted to him, followed him closely and noted his every action and word. Aisha had a unique opportunity to spend so much time with the Prophet and to learn his Sunnah. She spent nine years in the companionship of the Prophet Muhammad (pbuh) and during these nine years she gained a great deal of knowledge. She used to ask the Prophet many questions simply to enhance her own knowledge.

Aisha (ra) would sit inside her room and listen intently while the Prophet (pbuh) was teaching, talking or preaching sermons to his companions in the Masjid. At every opportunity, she would question the Prophet Muhammad (pbuh) and ask him to make things clear to her. She would persist with her probing until the matter was crystal clear to her. He would respond patiently, with the definite aim of moulding her mind and personality, as she was destined to convey and interpret his teachings to Muslims of all times.

According to a tradition of Aisha (ra), "whenever the Prophet had to choose between the two, he chose the easier option over the harder option." (Al-Bukhari)

Even the wisest mind cannot understand this, but she did. She explained that the Prophet (pbuh) said that in every situation in life, the human being has two choices in the way he handles that situation, the easier way or the harder. The harder way meant a violent option, while the easier way meant the peaceful option: the Prophet Muhammad (pbuh) always chose the easier option. If one chooses the violent (harder) option, it worsens the problem rather than solving it. Choosing the peaceful (easier) option provides an amicable solution. Only someone with her kind of intelligence and insight could understand the importance of this and explain it.

Aisha (ra) was a very intelligent lady and her conversation was full of wisdom. Many companions used to come to her to take her advice on a number of matters. Hazrat Mashrooq, who was the pupil of Aisha (ra), said: 'I had seen many important companions who were considerably older than Aisha (ra), but they used to come to her to have certain basic points of Islam made clear to them.'

Abu Musa states, 'Whenever there was an academic dispute, Aisha (ra) had a clear answer to it and the dispute was settled accordingly.'

Once she said, 'There is no better wealth one can take to Allah to meet Him than the least possible list of sins. The one who wants to excel in prayers should refrain from indulging in any kind of vices.'

Saad bin Hashaam states, 'I once requested Aisha (ra) to tell me something about the Prophet's habits and manners. She replied, 'Don't you read the Quran?'

I said, 'Yes of course.'

She said, 'The life of the Prophet Muhammad (pbuh) was the Quran personified, which means that whatever was prescribed in Quran, either to be followed or refrained from, was what the Prophet (pbuh) used to act upon very strictly.'

Aisha (ra) once referred to Safiyah (ra), one of the Prophet's (pbuh) other wives, as a midget. The Prophet (pbuh) immediately scolded her, "Aisha, what you have just said would pollute all the water of the sea!" "But that is a fact." she said. "True, but no amount of treasure will make me say such a thing about anyone."

Once the Prophet Muhammad (pbuh) heard Aisha (ra) cursing a thief for stealing something from her. He told her, "Aisha, don't take away from that person's sin and reduce your own reward by cursing!"

Prophet Muhammad (pbuh) also instructed her, 'If any poor comes to your door, don't refuse him alms, give him even if it is a piece of date. Aisha, love the poor and keep them near and dear to you so that you will be near to God on the Day of the Resurrection.'

Aisha (ra) also learned to read and write; a skill which was very rare among the male Arabs, let alone the females of those days. With great enthusiasm, she made full use of all her talents. She soon became proficient not only in religious knowledge but also in genealogy, history, literature and even in medicine.

She learned about different diseases and their remedies from the great physicians who used to visit the Prophet (pbuh). Every week she would give well worded lectures on Islam to people who gathered near her home for this purpose. Aisha (ra) was an outstanding speaker. Musa bin Talha was of the view that Aisha expressed herself really well.

The Prophet Muhammad (pbuh) displayed his affection and consideration for Aisha (ra) in many ways. Once during the Eid celebrations, some Africans were showing their skills with spears. She wanted to see their performance. He stood in front of her, while she watched over his shoulder. He kept standing there as long as she was interested in it.

The Prophet Muhammad (pbuh) and Aisha (ra) were once traveling with some of the Companions. At one point the Companions went ahead of them. He asked her to race with him. Aisha (ra) won the race easily. A few years later they raced again. This time the Prophet Muhammad (pbuh) won, as Aisha (ra) had put on some weight. Teasingly he commented, "Aisha, now we are even."

She loved the Prophet (pbuh) dearly, but her love for Allah SWT was much greater. Once, some hypocrites spread a rumour about her chastity. Although it caused great agony and grief to her and her dear ones, she was confident that Allah in His mercy would

protect her honour. Eventually, when the Divine revelation (24:11-20) confirmed her innocence, Umm Rumaan (ra) advised her daughter to touch the feet of the Messenger. Aisha (ra) refused, saying, "I do not worship anyone except Allah who has attested to my innocence and shamed the slanderers!"

After this revelation in which Allah SWT testified to her honesty, trustworthiness and purity, she became known as Siddiqa. Siddiqa means 'the truthful one'. Like her father, she always passionately upheld the truth. She never hesitated to speak the truth.

It was because of Aisha (ra) that the verse regarding the 'tayammum' (dry ablution) was revealed (4.43). This ayath (verse) lessened the hardship for all Muslims in the absence of water. She witnessed a number of revelations and had a clear understanding of the circumstances in which they were revealed.

The Prophet Muhammad (pbuh) and Aisha (ra) would often spend the night weeping and asking Allah's forgiveness in their 'tahajjud' (night prayers). The Prophet (pbuh) fasted frequently and so did Aisha (ra). During the last ten days of Ramadan he would be in the Masjid for 'itikaf'(seclusion) and Aisha (ra) would stay in her own tent in the Masjid's courtyard. She performed mid-morning prayers just as he did. All this training made her deeply pious.

It was the end of the month of Safar, 11A.H, when the Prophet Muhammad (pbuh) suddenly developed a severe headache. Soon after that he started running a high fever. In spite of his illness, he carried on with his regular routines, such as leading the 'salat' (prayers) and going to the house of each wife according to her turn. When his wives realized that his condition was deteriorating and he wished to be in Aisha's room, they gave up their turns and allowed him to stay with her during the final days of his life.

With the utmost devotion, Aisha (ra) nursed him day and night. His condition continued to worsen. One morning he made several attempts to get up and go to the Masjid un Nabi, but could not do so. In the end he said, "Tell Abu Bakr to lead the prayers!" Aisha (ra) pleaded, "Ya Rasool Allah, he is very soft-hearted, and will not be able to stand in your place and will burst into tears. Please order someone else to do so." Eventually, Abu Bakr (ra) had to lead the 'salat' as the Prophet (pbuh) insisted upon it.

In the 11 Hijri, the Prophet Muhammad (pbuh) breathed his last with Aisha (ra) at his side. He was laid to rest in her room. Thus she was blessed by Allah SWT in that she recorded the final moments of the last and the greatest Prophet.

Earlier, Aisha (ra) had related a dream to her father in which she had seen three moons falling in her room. After the burial of the Prophet (pbuh) he said, "He was the best of the three moons!" Her dream turned out to be true,

for later on Abu Bakr (ra) and Umar Farooq (ra) were also buried there.

After the death of the Prophet (pbuh), Aisha (ra) played an important role in carrying on his mission for almost fifty years. She devoted most of her time to the propagation of Islam and also took active part in education and social reform. She made every effort to spread Islam by teaching its tenets.

She used to educate people, and according to one estimate, she had about two hundred pupils, which included companions and the descendants of the companions as well.

Aisha (ra) held regular classes for both the young and the old. Her method of teaching was a combination of talk and discussion. At the end of the talk there would be a question and answer session. The orphans received special attention and she personally took care of all their expenses. She loved her students dearly; especially the orphans, and everyone respected and loved her in return.

Some of her students became great scholars of Islamic Law and Hadith. For example, her nephew Urwah became a distinguished reporter of hadith. Among her women pupils is the name of Umrah bint Abdur Rahman. She is regarded by scholars as one of the trustworthy narrators of hadith and is said to have acted as Aisha's (ra) secretary, receiving and replying to letters addressed to her.

Aisha (ra) performed Hajj every year. Her tent became the most inspiring place during her stay. People from far and wide and even from foreign countries came to get answers to their questions from her. She was the soul of politeness and would encourage the shy ones, saying, "You can freely ask me any question that you would ask your own mother."

She explained and interpreted complex matters to students and scholars. There was not a scholar of Hadith who did not directly benefit from her wisdom and knowledge. Even senior Companions, including Umar Farooq (ra), frequently turned to her for rulings on difficult matters. At the time of 'Hajjat al-Wadaa' (the Farewell Hajj) the Prophet (pbuh) said, "Learn some of your 'deen' (faith) from this red-haired lady." meaning Aisha (ra).

Her generosity also had no bounds. Often her allowance or any gifts of food that she received was distributed immediately to the needy the very same day, without her keeping any for herself. Although she herself was childless, she brought up several orphans and paid for their marriage expenses as well.

After getting married, one of the Companions wanted to give a 'walima' (a wedding dinner) but he did not have means to do so. The Prophet (pbuh) asked Aisha (ra) to send a basket of grains to him. Immediately, she sent to him whatever was at home and did not even keep anything for their evening meal, thus showing her obedience and generosity.

Being so generous, Aisha (ra) never turned down the request of a needy person. Once she was given a gift of one hundred thousand dirhams. She was fasting when she received the money and she distributed the entire amount to the poor and the needy even though she had nothing left in her house. Later a maidservant said to her: "Could you not buy meat for a dirham with which to break your fast?" "If I had remembered, I would have done so," she said. She was so preoccupied with serving others that she even forgot herself and her personal needs.

Before Abu Bakr (ra) passed away, he asked Aisha (ra) if she would forego her share in their property in favour of her much younger siblings. She did not hesitate for a moment and agreed to give up her share. Besides being generous, she was highly unselfish. When Umar Farooq (ra) was on his death bed, he sent his son Abdullah to her. He was to beg for her permission for Umar (ra) to be buried beside his beloved Prophet (pbuh). She wept saying, "I wanted to save this spot for my own grave, but I prefer Umar (ra) to myself."

As she grew older, she became one of the most beloved and respected persons in Arabia. At the age of 67, she suddenly fell ill in the month of Ramadan. People just poured in to find out how she was doing. By the time

Aisha breathed her last on 17, Ramadan, night had fallen. In shock, crowds gathered on the streets.

The same night the funeral prayer for her was led by Abu Huraira (ra). This was attended by thousands of people, who had never been seen before. She was buried in 'Baqee' (a graveyard near Masjid un Nabi) in accordance with her wishes.

Aisha (ra) was an extraordinary woman. She was a brilliant scholar and a teacher. She was the teacher of scholars and experts. She could understand better than any the deeper meaning and implications of what the Prophet Muhammad (pbuh) said. A good deal of information about important matters of faith came to the Ummah (Community) through her. Abu Musa Ashari once remarked that he received guidance from Aisha (ra) even in very complex matters. According to Imam Azhari, the knowledge possessed by Aisha (ra) outweighed the entire body of knowledge possessed by all of the Prophet's companions. Urwa bint

Zubair was of the opinion that nobody matched Aisha in her command of law, medicine and poetry.

The Ahadith, or sayings of the Prophet were handed down to posterity thanks mainly to four persons who transmitted more than two thousand of his sayings. Aisha (ra) is one of those four, the others being Abu Huraira (ra), Abdullah ibn Umar (ra), and Anas ibn Malik (ra). Aisha herself narrated about 2200 ahadith — an amazing achievement for a lady who was born before the dark ages. She became an inspiration for men and women alike!

May Allah be pleased with her. Ameen.

Illustrated by Gurmeet
First published 2018
Reprinted 2019
© Goodword Books 2019

Goodword Books
1, Nizamuddin West Market, New Delhi-110013,.
Tel. +9111-41827083, Mob. +91-8588822672
email: info@goodwordbooks.com
www.goodwordbooks.com

Goodword Books, Chennai
Mob. +91-9790853944, 9600105558

Printed in India